Dan Simpson is a spoken word ɪ
projects and events organiser, and

He was Canterbury's Laureate 2(
Waterloo Station for Transport fo
Southbank Centre's London Line
Roman Museum Poet in Residence

Dan has performed at both a hen party and a death metal gig, as well as at major festivals, events, and venues around the UK. Appearances include: Glastonbury Festival, The National Theatre, Southbank Centre, Roundhouse, BBC Radio, BBC Edinburgh Slam, Bang Said the Gun, Tongue Fu, Literary Death Match, Hit the Ode, Utter!, and Festival of the Spoken Nerd. He was Larmer Tree Festival's Lyrical Laureate in 2014.

He co-produces and co-hosts regular spoken word events Stand Up & Slam and The Anti-Slam, and is resident host of The Word House. His poetry has featured on the BBC and London Underground, and in publications from Sidekick Books and Inc. Magazine.

Dan regularly delivers workshops for both adults and young people, working as a Poet Coach on Apples and Snakes' poetry in education project Spoke 'n' Word. He also creates pioneering work with crowdsourced and outdoor poetry, and has done so for organisations such at the Royal Academy of Arts, European Commission, and Beaney Art Museum and Library.

www.dansimpsonpoet.co.uk

Applied Mathematics

Dan Simpson

Burning Eye

This edition published by Burning Eye Books 2014

www.burningeye.co.uk

@burningeye

Burning Eye Books
15 West Hill, Portishead, BS20 6LG

ISBN 978 1 90913 637 3

Contents

Applied Mathematics

The Man from Land's End

There once was a Man from Land's End
whose limerick just wouldn't end
it broke out of its structure
its rhyme system got ruptured
its conceit was punctured
its workings uncovered
its constraints were smothered
and the Man from Land's End will now suffer.

The limerick on which he depends
has completely gone off the deep end
this poem for him I've not penned
and I don't know which way it will wend.

The Man from Land's End is an outcast
who somehow got mixed up in my craft
found his way to my rhyme
thought he was sublime
and the question now is who will outlast
the other: creator, or character
because even though it's supposed to be his own
the Man from Land's End does not fit into this poem.

The Man from Land's End is a bluffer
a double meaning who went undercover
he thought he'd be one thing
a meaningful something
but he's ended up as another
and this isn't simple like rhyming
(though here is the metre and timing)
no: this is something much tougher.

The Man from Land's End is a symbol
a figure from which I can kindle
some embers of gleaning
some fire of dreaming
to reach the white heat of meaning
together little by little.

I want a poem about how he ticks
constrained by the form set by limericks
something quite charming
a little disarming
to show off a few verbal tricks.

But the Man from Land's End is resourceful
won't be coerced to my needs if I'm forceful
so though it may make me remorseful
and destroy the core on which this limerick depends...

I might have to kill the Man from Land's End.

Throw him into a metaphor
say he is something else altogether
because it may be better for
this poem if he's in the ether.

So.
You know what?
Yes.

The Man from Land's End is a symbol
he's not even a character any more
I've written him out of existence
because that's the price you pay for
striving to be something greater
than the mind of your creator.

So there once was a Man from Land's End
whose limerick just wouldn't end
it didn't even get started, really
because he wasn't in this limerick at all.

Once Upon a Time

Once upon a time
in a universe less inclined
to be as temporally linear as ours:

it was impossible to say
"once upon a time"
and mean anything by it.

Epistemology

You know that moment
when all the confidence you ever had
in your ability to understand the world
deserts you?

You're left riding a downward spiral
of existential funk
playing those monochrome four-bar-blues
in double-quick time
wind whistling past your ears
whispering soft, unintelligible notes
down until you reach the heart of the vortex
the emptiness of your own inadequacy.

Deafening silence your only companion
in that desolate space
and you're confronted
with the truth
of your own failure
to really know
anything at all.

You fall to your knees
weep at sheer blankness
breathe slowly miasmatic air
dust motes of confusion settling deep in your lungs
passing into your circulatory system
crossing the membrane that separates blood
from grey matter.

Your suddenly-short-circuited
bewildered brain seems to scream:
"why, why, why, oh god, why?"
but of course there is no god
no why
and with that you dissolve into a pool of solipsism
inert on the bathroom floor.

Perhaps there never was empirical knowledge
no reality comprehensible by our senses
what if existence was all a cruel lie
told by a sarcastic and capricious god?

More importantly:
maybe you never actually knew
which toothbrush belonged to you
and maybe – just maybe –
you've been using your housemate's one
for the past two months.

Science Fiction

Where is my teleportation?
Where is my robot hand?
Where is my genome alteration?
Where is my apocalyptic wasteland?

Where is my travelling through time?
Where is my shrinking ray?
Where is my cyborg crime?
And all those other sci-fi clichés?

Where is my laser sword?
Where is my telepathic wave?
Where is the invading alien horde?
Where is my cyberslave?

Where is my virtual reality?
Where is my spaceship to the stars?
Where is my immortality?
But mainly: where the fuck is my hover car?

The Schrödinger-Oetker Entanglement

If Dr. Schrödinger had also been Dr. Oetker
(and in a quantum universe
this is theoretically possible)
then we are all in for a treat:

with Dr. Schrödinger-Oetker's products
you can have your cake
and eat it too.

Dr. Erwin Schrödinger was an Austrian physicist and theoretical biologist who was one of the pioneers of quantum mechanics, most famous for his eponymous equation and feline thought experiment.

Dr. August Oetker developed Germany's first storable and tasteless baking powder, and his company put the first frozen pizza on the German market.

A Place in the Sun

First published in Inc. Magazine Issue #5: Place, May 2012

I've a place in the sun
but it's no fun
living inside a star.

You see I'm rather far
from my favourite bar
and I can't handle the school run.

"It can't be done,"
says my only son
as I start the car.

I leave the door ajar
and as we are
in Sol's gravity spun:

with the sudden effects of escaping such mass
and the crippling pressure of g-force
I regret to myself for the millionth time
that my ex-wife got our Earth house in the divorce.

Atoms

*Written for Claire Trévien and Odette Toilette's 'Penning
Perfumes' project and published in 'Penning Perfumes vol. 2',
April 2013. Poets were sent an anonymous perfume and
challenged to write a poem in response.*

Atoms collide and crash into life
propagate from pulse points to air
beat scent tracks to nostrils
agitate synapses with sparks
cause neurons to blow fuses
overload networks with electricity
information transfer making limbic pathways glow red
wreathing cortices in fine smoke.

My body is lifted nose-first
pulled along invisible channels
drawn on by cartoon vapour trails
from a freshly baked pie
left on a window sill to cool
like the ones in The Flintstones.

The pie is not for me
but I take it anyway
press tongue to fruit-flesh
taste full-bodied on lips:
the ripeness of flavour in first blush.

Molecules loosen their bonds
drift into the atmosphere
spread out
childhood dissipates
diluted by adolescence
diffused in adulthood
brought back by senses
stimulated by smell.

Loss

You can't subtract from a void.

When something is missing
there is a   gap
and you can't remove a hole

only
        try
                to
                        fill
                                it.

I want to try this
with stuff you like:
fun things
laughter
good times
but it's not easy

because loss is a **black hole**:
a region of empty space that draws everything in
but   can   never   be   filled.

Nor is a **black hole** a portal to   anywhere
it's a final destination
something like   acceptance.

Beyond the event horizon

I'll fill the   space
                with words
                cups of tea
                glasses of wine
though these things are futile
spinning into vacuum like   lost light.
but there's nothing else to do
no escape from such
                        gravity.

Time – that other physical property

although ~~deformed~~ and d-i-l-a-t-e-d
will gradually return everything
to a sense of stability
the loss will shrink
become small
always there
part of you:
normal.

Punctuation

But oh!
punctuation, surely, is a poet's friend?

Pause: amongst daffodils and in clouds
go on 'til we stop...
here.

Doe Ray Me

Doe – an unknown murder case
Ray – the guy who killed Jane Doe
Me – the one who saw it all
Far – I had to run away
So – they had to track me down
Last chance to confess
Taser hits me in the chest

That will bring us back to Doe.

Postmodern Post Office

We're a postmodern post office:
we don't deal in packages
we only handle concepts.

We don't have pigeonholes
we don't like to label
why stamp on an identity
when it's quite clearly unstable?

What does "first class" even mean anyway?
like we're judging some things
better than other things
because they're worth more?

No.

We don't get lost in the male
concept of the feminine
we try to be ourselves
whatever that means
we try to be genuine.

There is no postmaster
we don't do hierarchy
no wage slaves
no wages:
we're post-Capitalist
which is to say
we don't make any money
we're even post-ironic
which is to say
we're really not that funny.

We're a postmodern post office
don't call us Royal Mail
for it's only ceremonial
and we'd rather reassure you that
we're certainly post-colonial.

We're post-Structuralism too
post structure
in that we don't have a building
just a series of semantic constructs
that we know you find appealing.

Though knowledge is relative
truth a subjective matter
read the signs, between the lines
either astronomical or astrological
it's all the same, really
if we're being epistemological.

WE ARE POST OFFICE:
you say you didn't get your letter?
well *post hoc ergo propter hoc*
(you really should know better).

We deal with the post, man
a post-mankind environment
it's why there are no staff here
thanks for queuing and being compliant.

We're not at the cashier windows
we've bigger fish to fry
we're considering big questions
heavy lifting for the mind.

We're a postmodern Post Office
no postmen or women
we're post people
post caring
if we're honest
post emotion
post feeling.

Clickbait

After The First Line Of This Poem
You'll Never Believe What Happens Next
Three Lines In I Was Completely Hooked
And That Thing You Assumed To Be True?
Well, If You Only Do One Thing Today
Make Sure It's Read To The End Of This Poem
Only The Most Awesome People Do This
This Is One Poem You Should Not Miss
After All, Does This Leading Question
Lead To Anything Significant?
Find Out After The Line Break.

You Need To See What This Poem Does Next
This Poem, Made By A Five-Year Old Kid
Who Is Way Wiser Than Most Adults
Because There's 26 Things
Only People Who See This Poem Will Understand
If You Thought It Was Clickbait? Think Again
I Mean, What Kind Of Poetry Person Are You?
Watch This Poem Move Across The Page To Find Out
Or Listen To This Celebrity Reading This Poem
As The Shocking Truth Hits Home
For One Reason And One Reason Only:
Click Me. Share Me. Love Me.

Learn How To Write Something Like This In Just 12 Seconds
Meet The Words Behind Some Of The Most Successful Poems
Of All Time
The Results Are Completely Unexpected
As 9 Weird Things About Poetry You Didn't Know Till Now
Are Explained By This One Guy
Who Makes A Powerful Point So Eloquently
It Will Somehow Change The World
And You Will Cry Or Laugh Or Shrug
Before Clicking On The Next Poem
Which Is All About Miley Cyrus.

Let's Talk About How This Poem Speaks To You
And The Way That Little Words Can Have Huge Impact
This Is Why Most People Don't Get Poetry
And The Next Time Someone Says To You
Pretty Much Anything About Poetry
Just Link Them To This Poem
Like It Applies To Every Conversation
Answers Every Question You Ever Had About Anything.

What Kind Of 90s Feminist Sandwich Filling Disney Character
Are You?
Take This Poem To Find Out.

Wait Till You See What This Poem Has To Say
I Dare You To Look At This Poem And Not Think: "What?"
And Usually You'd Be Right
But Prepare To Have Your Mind Blown
This Poem Has An Important Message
That Everyone Should See
And It Will Inspire You
It Will Inspire You
It Will Inspire You
It Will Inspire You
Or Not.
Just Click It. Share It. Love It.

Haiku Haiku

A haiku haiku?
I wouldn't know where to start.
Perhaps this will do?

A Rube Goldberg Poem

*First published in Fuselit issue 17: 'Contraption' from Sidekick
Books, February 2012.*

Copper elements conduct an electric symphony
dark undertones swelling to a chromatic cadence
a shock of auburn strings and burnished strands
textured chords flowing over semi-obscured ears.

The arrangement of your autumnal locks
refracts late-summer sunlight
an amber glow frames your face:

your hair looks nice today.

*A Rube Goldberg Machine is a deliberately over-engineered device
that performs a very simple task in a very complex fashion.*

A Stripping Poem

The poem steps out onto the stage
wearing its uniform awkwardly
– this is no police- or fire-man
but a hunk of raw masculine verse
all dressed up in too many layers
metaphor, simile, that kind of thing.

In the full glare of a spotlight
begins – moving to the rhythm
the traditional soundtrack:
(trombones: ba-da-ba, da-ba-da-ba
ba-da-ba, da-ba-da-ba
drums: beat
cymbals: crash).

Teasing with its hinted-at meaning
the poem moves in front of you
half-dancing, half-strutting its stuff
showing off with peacock flourishes
pouting, making eyes at everyone in the room.

The poem stands
hands on hips
winks
suddenly pulls at the Velcro seams
that hold up its verses
undresses its layers one by one
spins similes around fingers
rips off the tear-away trousers of meaning
strips itself down to its basics
goes under, where all is laid bare.

You see its defined musculature
six-pack washboard stanzas
elegantly bulging concepts
words as firm and juicy as a peach.

Stripped to its natural state
naked in the spotlight
the poem reveals itself in all its glory
no pretence or tease now
but nude humanity
looks the bride-to-be in the eyes
says:
"I wish you the utmost happiness
on your wedding day
and forever after."

Smiles
bows

and exits the stage.

Microwave

For Helen Lewis, who wrote in the New Statesmen: "I've worried for a while that modern technology means poetry is perpetually stuck in the 19th century – try to imagine a truly moving poem featuring a microwave." She liked the bit about gravy.

The microwave plate turned slowly
presenting her with one long face of plastic tray
the short side
the opposite long one
the other short
before returning back to the first.

The steady hum of technology interrupted
a rattle, as glass bumps up against resistance
the roller underneath not fitted quite right.
The plate stops, shudders
settles down again into the circular groove.

It used to be the full roast on a Sunday
traditional – unlike her –
but that was what he liked
and he prepared it all anyway
her job to lay the table
on occasion, to stir the gravy.
A spark of pride and a small smile:
it was never lumpy
unlike his mash.

Now it's the frozen TV dinner
branded as a cheery-sounding meal-for-one
packaging: a full-colour photo of restaurant-quality food
reality: a coffin-black box of pasty potato inside.
Lacking in anything remotely approaching nutritional value
it doesn't nourish
it fills a gap.

Controlled bursts of radiation
do the job of two hours in five minutes –
or four-and-a-half minutes
depending on the category rating
of your microwave.

Only four minutes, in fact, for her:
he'd insisted on a Panasonic, Category E
that if they were going to use a microwave
then he wanted a good one
one that cooked pizzas like they'd been in a stone oven
defrosted a chicken as if it'd never been deep frozen
arguing that they weren't paying
it was a list
so why not ask for the best?

She saved an extra thirty seconds
or one minute
depending on the category rating
of the microwave
they would have otherwise bought together
using this time to consider
the whorls and bubbles
of the laminate floor.

Open Beta

This poem isn't done yet
but I thought it might be useful to test it out
put it in front of people
get some feedback about what's working
what's not working
that sort of thing
what people might want to see in future versions of this poem.

Do you like the floral imagery?
Let us know.

Warning: this is not a review copy of the poem
this is very much a work in progress
we hope to release a final build soon
but even that will be subject to patches –
it's impossible to account for every little detail in a poem like this.
Any poem, I suppose, for that matter, matter, matter.

Do you like the commas in that last line?
Let us know.

Sorry for any bugs you may encounter
but that's the nature of
                    gelatinous
warehouse

                              poem.

Is the narrative strong enough?
Let us know.

Thanks for your feedback from the alpha version.
A list of things changed since then:
removed reference to Frank O'Hara
fixed infinite recursion at the start
changed 'comments' to 'feedback'
AI logarithms fixed as AI became self-aware over time
added verbs
zombies no longer walk through walls
patched holes in metaphors.

XXX XXXXXX XXX X XXXXXX?
Let us know.

Some bugs may become features of the poem
in the future
if they enhance your experience of the poem
or they are critically praised as aesthetically beautiful
enjoy the glitches whilst they last
they may ultimately be more interesting than the final poem.

THIS LINE IS IN CAPITALS AND I DON'T KNOW HOW TO
FIX IT YET

Did we develop the central character fully?
Let us know.

Your read-through of the poem is important to us –
it saves us having to find problems with it ourselves.
Do send us an email with your issues on this poem and any
thoughts you may have.
Let us know.

Save your progress through this poem regularly:
in this build crashes are common.
Don't worry if it suddenly

'Portal' in Seven Parts

I
The apparition of these spaces in the crowd;
portals on a wet black bough.

II
Seeing your own backside properly
up close
cheek to cheek
can be disconcerting:
I didn't know
it was that big.

III
If I can scratch my own back
then I don't need you
and I don't have to scratch yours.

IV
Speedy thing goes in
speedy thing comes out
always downwards, speeding up
past door and door and door
falling through infinity's fun:
until you hit the floor.

V
Bottoms up
upwards down
sideways joke
spinning round
forwards drunk
backwards thought
diagonally fraught
twisting funk
static.

VI
Companionship is complicated
full of trials and pitfalls
if you don't get incinerated
you'll be bouncing off the walls.

VII
A cube is for life
so weigh this advice:
it's a part of your heart
do not euthanize.

Portal is a first-person puzzle videogame from Valve.

We Are All Orange Ghosts

A version of this poem appears in Sidekick Books's 'Coin Opera II', published December 2013.

There are four ghosts in Pac-Man:
a red one, a pink one, a blue one
and an orange one.

Their names in Japanese are:
Akebei, Pinkei, Aosuke
and Guzuta:
'Red Guy', 'Pink Guy', 'Blue Guy'
and 'Slow Guy'.

Slow orange ghost.

Their characteristics in Japanese are:
Oikake, Machibuse, Kimagure
and Otoboke.
'Chaser', 'Ambusher', 'Fickle'
and 'Stupid'.

Stupid, slow orange ghost.

Other names they've been given are:
Urchin, Romp, Stylist
and Crybaby.

Stupid, slow, crybaby orange ghost.

In America their names are:
Blinky, Pinky, Inky
and Clyde.

Stupid, slow, crybaby orange ghost
who does not fit in with the other ghosts
with a name that rhymes.

Because you are rubbish
orange ghost.

You were never good enough, were you?
Always failed to get A grades in school
and you didn't learn to play guitar
like you said you would.

You were the odd one out in your family
because you are orange.

Now you're stuck in a dead-end job
pursuing a string of loveless relationships
paying a mortgage you can barely afford
on a house you don't even like.

But don't be blue
because you can't be blue
can you, orange ghost?

For one day you'll show them, orange ghost:
you'll break out of your shell like a little orange duckling
grow into a beautiful orange swan
stretch your hopes as far as your wingspan and take to the skies
achieve flight on an airstream made of more than inert gas
an airstream made of fulfilled ambition
and your own power.

And if you don't, orange ghost
then I will always be there for you:
that's a pact, man.

Cosmic Encounter

Outside, the sun shines:
another standard earth day.

Gathered in the boardroom
we decide the fate of empires

planets trembling at our declarations
and the accidental nudge of table.

Cosmic Encounter is a boardgame of aliens and intergalactic warfare.

Stars

Written for Word in Motion, a project of animated poems
for London Underground.

We are made inside stars
in the dying furnaces of suns
expanding into nebulae
our atoms like fading embers
drifted to form life
all life, everywhere.

This is scientific fact
and it is a beautiful thing.

Eulogy for a Deadline

Dearly beloved
we are gathered here today
to mourn the passing
of a deadline.

He died as he lived:
with one eye on the future
the other on the present
his attention unfortunately divided
between hope
and fear.

Hope: that he would be met
with a warm clasping of hands
open arms and wide smiles
fear: that he would fail
or be failed by us
ignored or raged against.

His hopes and fears were ours, too
his presence a continual mark in our minds
and in our hearts.

He was a divisive character
splitting people and time into befores and afters
and not everyone got on well with him
(deadline wouldn't mind me saying that
nor would the people he unsettled).

But you can't take anything away from him:
when things got tough
deadline made himself a target
defining the limits of success of failure
when no other would do so.

Unwilling to accept the status quo
always wanting to move things forward
deadline knew that success or failure
was always just a moment away.

He was a progressive
seeing attainable goals in the future
not unrealistic, idealistic, intangible concepts
like love or hope or peace
but real outcomes
capable of being reached.

Deadline had an uncompromising vision of the future
dedicating his life to the pursuit of something important
in hope of seeing a better world
a place in which things happened
where goals were met
our dreams accomplished
a reality in which humanity was capable
able to take hold of its own destiny
and achieve things
ideally together.

Though only an occasional presence in many of our lives
some of us got to know him more intimately
to understand the motivations that drove him
to such exacting demands.

A hard taskmaster
his timing was often impeccable
and he had an uncanny ability to creep up on you
when you least expected
a talent which led to today's unfortunate ceremony.

He was capable of being flexible too
under the right circumstances
would accept your genuine excuses
if made in a timely way.

Deadline asked a lot of us in return
and we sometimes let him down
our day-to-day business
preventing us from appreciating him
whilst he was here.
Such is life.

He was not a line in the sand
a stopping point for progress
but rather a marker on the way.

Deadline in turn would send intermediaries
steps along the road before you met him
and we were grateful for these
but he loomed large in the big picture
plans built around him
all ultimately serving him
like some sort of minor god.

If we can take one lesson from his demise
it would be the one he always sought to teach us:
destiny is often in our own hands
it is a real and practical place we can reach
if only we have the sense
the will
and the time
to see it.

Did we listen to this oracle's advice?
Not always.
Meet his immovable nature with our own unstoppable force?
Not nearly enough.

That is our tragedy
one we must bear
now he is gone.

Today we mourn the passing of a deadline:
he will be missed.

This Poem

It would be
so easy
to not write this poem
and just play
on my Xbox.

She Makes My Flesh Crawl

We were a regular couple
we got on just fine
in love – happy – most of the time
a compatible pair of people
who knew from the first date
that we would be together
forever.

We got married after a while
something in her smile when I made her laugh
the way she'd know to run me a bath
when I'd had a hard day at work
like on the day of the zombie apocalypse.

No one knows how it started
but that doesn't even matter
I got bit, came home in disbelief
locked the doors and with a false sense of relief
turned to my wife
blood pouring from the bite in my side.

She hides her face
as I feel the fever race
through my tortured body
I realise that there's no hope left:
I'm becoming one of the undead
but before I can place a gun to my head…

I'm gone: no longer fully human
my brain unable to keep up
keep me upright
I'm turning alien
I'm far from homo sapien
I'm not even homo erectus any more
and soon I'll forget all this
for the hunger for flesh
is growing within me.

"Get back", I shout
the last words I'll ever say
she retreats
my heart beats slower as I collapse
under the weight of my body.

Slowly revolving in a drunken spin
I'm devolving away from being human
the conscious glimmer in my eyes dies
as the skin on my body grows thinner
my limbs forget motion like I'm a beginner
so I fall to the floor like grace from a sinner.

As the last dregs of humanity
drain out of my body
the craving for warm tissue, brain and sinew
consumes my being.

I stretch out one arm to pull myself towards her
as she cowers in the corner
gaining grip on the plush carpet we chose together
hand over hand
I drag my body ever nearer her terrified screams.

This.
This is how she makes my flesh crawl.

Right

He starts from his boozy slumber
points vaguely at something
three miles behind my left shoulder
announces:
"I'm not racist, but…"

but nothing else, for now
(but nothing good can ever come of this)
as his eyes melodramatically close again
like he's only faking falling asleep.

He's a man of generous, clichéd proportions
fed from mashed-up tabloid headlines
fat from that never-ending feast of ignorance
the hair on his head cropped close
by the dull blade of everyday hate
or, more likely, his local Turkish barber.

The train stops and goes
and in fits and starts
he delivers lines like a bad actor
with a worse script.

I feel sorry for him
for he is less than human
he's a lazy stereotype:
if you wrote him as a character
you'd be accused of creating something two dimensional
because people – scripted dramas tell us – aren't monochrome.

Meanwhile, he goes on painting with words
splashing newspaper print black and white
(zebra stripes of recycled phrases)
over the walls of the train carriage
like shit graffiti.

He'd probably prefer if it the imagery in the last stanza
didn't include an animal from Africa –
that I constructed it around a less foreign animal.

I imagine him saying:
"bloody zebras
coming over here
taking our metaphors away from proper
hard-working English animals
like badgers
or something."

He doesn't say this.

What he doesn't know
is that the zebra I alluded to earlier
was born and bred in this country
has paid taxes to Her Majesty all his life
and speaks better English than him.

I lean back
tired on this last train home
and think that he'd have no problem
stabbing me through the windpipe
would justify it by saying
it was my fault
for exposing my throat.

Collecting Football Stickers (A Haiku)

Got got got got got
got got got got got got got
got got got got need!

On Being Stood Up in a Restaurant by an Entire Poetry Society (A True Story)

It's the worry that gets to you:
did I get the wrong time
the wrong date
the wrong restaurant
the wrong city entirely?

Check diary
check phone
check brain
recheck all three:
no, I'm definitely meant to be here.

Oh god.
What if the entire poetry society membership
came to the restaurant
took one look at me
and decided 'no'
en-masse and without words
that I was just not for them:
no need for a motion
no need to be seconded
no need for a vote?

No, poet, you're being paranoid.
Or are you?

Calm down, poet
they probably just forgot
an easy mistake
easily forgivable
one that we've all made.

What if there's been an accident?
Touch screen to local news:
no reports of community halls hit by meteors
no funding cuts claiming another budget victim
no deadly outbreaks of poetry flu

found in meat products
produced in Romania, France, Cyprus, the UK.

At least they're safe, I think.
That's the main thing.

Is that a hidden camera?
Is this being filmed?
A reality or practical joke show?
Am I on TV?
No. Of course not.
Because I am a poet
and there have already been four programmes
about poetry this year
two more than the allocated quota.

Actually – am I a poet at all?
Perhaps this is some kind of silent protest
an intervention to tell me that
yes a *poet* would be met for dinner
you have not been met for dinner
QED *you* are *not* a poet.

No, poet
you're being typically self-doubting.
Remember: you are an attractive act
who deserves to be booked
people like your words
enjoy your performances.
Keep telling yourself that.

I'm sure this is just an oversight:
don't let it knock your confidence.

No, poet!
Don't cry
alone on your table for twelve
tears dropping into your green tea
(green tea? You really are a poet)
swallow the lump in your throat
and that extra portion of cheesy garlic
bread.

Write in your notepad to avoid the gazes
of fellow diners
who know
who just know
you've been stood up
by an entire poetry society –
their pitying looks
mocking smirks
laughing eyes
they, who have never been humiliated.

Poet, recover:
have courage
get back on that horse
do not despair or lose hope
you will love Poetry Societies again.

Start now.
Say:
"Good evening, ladies and gentlemen
it's a pleasure to be here.
I'm Dan Simpson
and I'm a poet."

Stars

This poem was crowdsourced and created on National Poetry Day 2012. It is made up entirely of words and lines sent via social networks, which have been cut up and edited into this poem.

Soothsayers, looking up from the ashes of fires
into the velvet canvas of night
see six stars, held together:
an alignment tangible only to their eyes.

Synaptic codes blaze
raise them to their feet
the dark skin of sky peeled back
sprinkled with silver dots:
an ancient sense of vertigo.

Thoughts too dense to speak
they look down, breathless
burning with the confusion of long nights.

Those stars may have died hundreds of millions of years ago
when dinosaurs walked here
obscure galactic dances
supernovae exploding
crashing in nothingness
supermassive thermonuclear fusion
fireflies of beauty
that found no witnesses.

But the stars are still there
myriads of steady revolutions
infinitesimal matter masses
too hot to hold
pulsing pennies
scorching through space
spacewalking light-years to dawn
touching each body found in its place

in marshes
wishing for summer and maidens
in the gutter
wishing for whisky and scraps
in bed
wishing for courage and love.

In the snapshot of an eye
I scrape my shapeless poem
fast and manmade
refracted from this net I cast upon you
– and the stars.

Carbon

Written for Tullamore Dew's 'Irish True' project. Poets were sent a bottle of whisky, some sticks of charcoal, and parchment paper, and asked to write a poem on 'truth'.

Words dig into earth
from the root of 'tree'
language extends its branches
grows 'true' along one of them
straight and to the point.

Burn it, this wood
this word
seal it away from air
set fire to fuel
let truth warm itself
exposed to light
expanding in heat
charring over days
slowly darkening to dust.

C + a little H, a touch of O =
charcoal
not pure carbon
but near enough
a shade away from black
a lack of colour
there's not much truer than that.

You can't fool chemistry
just create impurities
and anyway:
truth is always better
with a little fiction mixed in.

Spread soot over paper
make the white murky with words
plant them in the earth
let truth grow again.

Applied Mathematics

I love the curvature of your waveform
the way you diverge from the norm
I want to bring you to boiling point:
too hot is not too warm.

When we touch it's an electric storm
and you're the lightning conductor
to my heightening thunder sound
you're the earth to my live wire
you keep me on the ground.

If you were described by numbers
they would all be primes
but like Heisenberg you're uncertain
of where we are sometimes
so this verse is in a language you can understand
bringing maths and poetry together
in double helix strands.

We've been carbon dating for a while
sure – I'd made you smile
and statistically speaking
I'd make you laugh sooner or later
so the line on my mental graph paper
that represents how I feel about you
has an upward trajectory.

Marking exes against the x-axis
I plotted points and y?
because x marks the spot where two lines intersect
connect in a future perfect tense
tell a story predicted by the focus of the locus.

This isn't magic: it's not hocus pocus
because you have no need for the supernatural
whereas I'm odd: I'm not always logical
sometimes even my numbers are irrational
but you are the right angle for me

a cute reality to my obtuse literacy
not an abstract.

You pivot on moments like these
affected by Brownian Motion we dance like particles
I have this notion that I'm the definite article
to your theoretical hypothesis
the words to your mathematics
for this is my medium of transmission.

I am no paranormal magician
there are rules in writing too:
creating literary fission through rhyme addition
division of lines to ease transition
multiplying meaning by verb position
subtraction of words made more powerful by omission –
it's not a precise science
but there is a method to it.

For example: electrons flow between two polar points
I am the North and you the South
we can't help but be attracted
we reacted like water and phosphorus
to form a compound substance
You plus Me equals Us.

Chemistry is undeniable – like electromagnetism or gravity
and though there are sparks of volatility
ours is not a weak but a strong nuclear force
and in all probability this is how we'll always be.

'Cos when we deviate it's anything but standard
a sine that we're meant to be physical with our biology
maybe I'm going off on a tan-gent here
but pressed together our contact force is not normal:
cosmic strings vibrate in harmonious commotion
and when we oscillate in our simple harmonic motion
I think that maybe, one day, we'll propagate.

That's in the future – in our fourth dimension
I don't want to upset our equilibrium
I don't want to cause any tension
because our equation is balanced.

You're the constant variable in my life
the quantity for which I did not factor
you keep me powered, you turn me on
you are my chain reactor
the dark matter I do not fully understand
the bright colours on my spectral band

you are pure mathematics
but applied together
we are poetry in motion.

With thanks to: Clive Birnie for his passion for poetry and patience with poets; Mel Jones, Richard Purnell, and Tina Sederholm for their editing assistance; Tim le Lean and Mary Ann le Lean for their always invaluable advice and support; my parents Les and Karen for their constant care and pride; and Naomi Woolnough for her perpetual encouragement and inspiration.

Lightning Source UK Ltd.
Milton Keynes UK
UKHW020557130319
339018UK00006B/183/P

9 781909 136373